HOW TO FIND WORK THAT YOU LOVE —

When You're Stuck in a Job That You Hate

— A Life Guide —

HOW TO FIND WORK THAT YOU LOVE —

When You're Stuck in a Job That You Hate

— A Life Guide —

Dr. Suzanne Gelb, PhD, JD

FIRST EDITION

All rights reserved. This book or any portion thereof may not be reproduced or used in any manner whatsoever without the express written permission of the publisher except for the use of brief quotations in a book review.

Copyright © 2019 Dr. Suzanne J. Gelb, Ph.D., J.D.

Manufactured in the United States of America.

ISBN-13: 978-1-950764-04-4
ISBN-10: 1-950764-04-4

www.DrSuzanneGelb.com

PRAISE FOR... THE LIFE GUIDES

I wrote this life guide on how to find work that you love, along with 10 other life guides on various topics, to help readers successfully navigate some of life's trickiest challenges.

Each Life Guide includes educational information sourced from my three+ decades of coaching and counseling in the field of emotional wellness.

What Readers Are Saying

"You know when people say, 'Just visualize your job interviewer in her underwear... and no one will be able to tell how nervous you are?' Unfortunately, that's not quite true.

As a former Human Resources consultant, I can tell you: you need to be clear, confident and self-assured at the hiring table, or you won't get the opportunity you want.

Your next step?

Dr. Suzanne Gelb's brilliant Life Guide on **How To Find Work That You Love.**

(While you're at it, considering purchasing all eleven Life Guides. They're all gems!)

You can have the career you want, but first, you have to learn how to manage your emotions so that you can make a terrific impression.

Bravo to Dr. Gelb for creating these incredibly valuable — and affordable — guidebooks. I wish I could have given a copy to everyone I ever interviewed."

—Susan Harrow, Media Coach and Marketing Strategist, Founder of PR Secrets, Bestselling Author of *Sell Yourself Without Selling Your Soul*

"As a career and business strategist, I know that finding great work isn't always easy. It takes passion and patience. It's a marathon — not a sprint!

Having a terrific resume (or business plan) is just part of the process. You also need to get your mindset in a positive mode — and get your emotions working for you, instead of against you.

Dr. Gelb's Life Guide on **"How to Find Work That You Love"** *is an indispensable road map to what is — for many — a grueling & challenging journey. Use this guide, and you'll have the tools that you need to move forward with confidence and grace."*

—Ellen Fondiler, Career and Business Strategist

"Your guidebooks are gems."

—Alexandra Franzen, Published Author, Writing Teacher

"Learning how to love yourself and treat yourself kindly — even when your life, career, body, and relationships aren't 'totally perfect' — is one of the hardest things to do.

Dr. Suzanne Gelb breaks down the art of self-love into practical steps. No woo-woo vagueness. Just easy-to-follow exercises pulled from her 28-year career in the field.

If you're looking for practicality and effectiveness, these Life Guides are a steal of a deal."

—Susan Hyatt, Master Certified Life Coach, Published Author

"Dr. Gelb has a gentle spirit that instantly makes you feel like you've come home. The depth of her wisdom is undeniable, her curiosity is insatiable and her love is palpable. These qualities make her the perfect guide for life.

In the pages of the Life Guides you will find practical and proven processes to support you in living your great life. Whether it's heart-centered wisdom on navigating the dating world, love-based strategies for becoming a parent, or reaching your ideal weight through kindness, Dr. Gelb's Life Guides are gifts to be treasured."

— Dr. Gemma Stone, Psychologist, Mentor, Published Author

CONTENTS

Disclaimer.   XV

INTRODUCTION

Change Your Work, Change Your Life.   1

WHAT'S INSIDE AND HOW TO USE THIS GUIDE.   4

STEP 1

What's Your Aspiration in Life?   5

STEP 2

What's NOT Working?   9

STEP 3

What IS Working?   16

STEP 4

Seeing ALL the Options.   24

STEP 5

What's Your Dream?   36

STEP 6

Make a Plan.   44

STEP 7

Keep Working ... For Love.   49

A FEW FINAL WORDS   53

MORE TIPS, MORE TOOLS

3 FAQs: Work / Career Challenges With a Fresh, Uplifting Spin   54

WHAT'S NEXT

Resources… to Help You Find Work That You Love
(And Stay Motivated and Inspired for the Journey...)   94

ABOUT THE AUTHOR   104

OTHER BOOKS BY THE AUTHOR   105

INDEX   107

DISCLAIMER

This book is a tool that can help you to find work that you love.

This book contains educational exercises and tips drawn from my career in the field of emotional wellness with over 30 years of experience. This book is for informational purposes only, and is not intended to diagnose or treat any illness, nor is it a substitute for professional or psychological advice, diagnosis, or treatment. Always consult a qualified health care professional before engaging in any new, self-help resource (such as this one) and with questions you may have about your health and wellbeing.

Any case material that may be alluded to in this book, including in articles, or in interviews [see Resources section] does not constitute guarantees of similar outcomes for the reader. No results can be promised, since everyone's personal development path is unique. Names and details have been changed for privacy.

Links inside this book to external websites are for informational purposes only. Linking does not imply endorsement of or affiliation with that site, its content, or any product or service it may offer.

All link URLs in this book are current at the time of printing. Link URLs may fail at some point if the page has been deleted or moved. The author assumes no responsibility or liability for broken links.

This concludes the disclaimer portion of this book.

Thank you. Enjoy this Guide ... and enjoy your life..

INTRODUCTION

Change Your Work, Change Your Life

Welcome to The Life Guide on How to Find Work That You Love.

If you're reading this Guide, chances are, **you're not feeling so great about your work.**

("Not so great" might be putting it mildly. You might even HATE it.)

Right now, you might be feeling like ...

— Your working environment is a prison. Draining your spirit, every single day.

— You chose the wrong industry, the wrong position, the wrong company, or the wrong business model, and now it's too late to change course.

— You're a smart person, but totally ... stuck. Overwhelmed. Unable to get moving and find the motivation to seek out something new.

— You know you're not living up to your potential, and time is running out, and it's All Your Fault.

— There simply aren't any other options for you. Or maybe there are, but you can't see them clearly.

— You're bound by your obligations and circumstances. (Kids, family, mortgage, debt, etc...) You just can't afford to take a risk, at this stage in the game.

Or, maybe ...

— You don't know exactly "why" you're unhappy with your job or career. You just are. Something's not right. And it's becoming too bothersome to ignore.

Whatever you're feeling, the good news is:

It is NEVER too late to learn something new — or choose a new path.

As a woman who holds five university degrees, and who has reinvented her career path, I'm living proof of that!

After moving through this Life Guide, my hope is that

— you'll be inspired to take those first few steps towards a more meaningful career (the first few are always the toughest!)

and that

— you'll feel better equipped to manage your fears and emotions, as your journey unfolds.

When you LOVE your work, you DO better work.

And the whole world **benefits** from your love.

Let's begin!

What's Inside and How To Use This Guide

Inside this Life Guide, you'll find a **series of steps** to guide you through uncovering your true career passion and figuring out the first steps to move closer to your dream work scenario.

Some steps include **fill-in-the-blank worksheets**.

Other steps contain **scripts** to help you **uplift your self-talk** – I know all too well how discouraging and frustrating this process can be, at times.

Each step is designed to help you not only

- **Step forward into work that's aligned with your deepest aspirations**

But to also

- **Deepen your trust in YOURSELF in the process.**

The Contents page gave you a peek at what's ahead:

STEP 1

What's Your Aspiration in Life?

In one of her hit singles, Beyoncé says:

"My aspiration in life? To be happy."

This international pop superstar is clearly an ambitious, talented, successful woman ... with a HUGE career.

And yet, her aspiration is very simple: "To be happy."

You might be thinking,

"Well, that's my aspiration too! Isn't it everyone's?"

But pause, just a moment.

Go deeper.

Your highest aspiration in life might actually be ... something else.

Maybe your aspiration in life is ...

To be helpful.

To be kind.

To experience peace of mind.

To prevent tragedies from happening — and make the world safer.

To be brutally honest and shake up the status quo.

To inspire others to take brave risks.

To entertain others — to make people laugh, cry and feel.

To have big adventures.

To be surrounded by beauty — in all forms.

To push your body to its physical limits.

To feel awake.

To feel useful.

To taste it all.

To be in love.

Before we start exploring what your next career move might be, we need to define your greatest aspiration in life.

Otherwise, you might choose a form of work that's misaligned with what you really desire. (Which is likely to lead to more dissatisfaction…)

Try to fill in the following blank, even if it means filling up lots and lots of pages with different phrases and ideas until …

You land on the one that **feels just right.**

You'll know when you're getting closer …

You'll feel it.

You'll know you're getting closer when you keep circling back to the same or a similar idea.

Don't question it.

Don't argue with it.

Just trust it.

My aspiration in life is to

_____

_____

_____

You don't have to be 100% clear about your aspiration, right this second.

And it's OK if you have **more than one aspiration,** too. Even a vague idea is better than NO idea at all.

Once you have even a TINY bit of clarity about what your highest aspiration might be, you can start to figure out what kind of work would be truly satisfying.

Hold onto that aspiration for the moment.

Next up?

Let's explore what's NOT working, when it comes to your current work.

STEP 2

What's NOT Working?

"I hate my work!"

Those are four words I've heard many times over the past 30+ years.

When a client is unhappy about their job or career, I often ask:

"What's NOT working, when it comes to your work?"

Some clients quickly rattle off a list of ten or twenty things that:

- Bother them
- Stress them out
- Feel misaligned with their values

or

- Feel boring and meaningless.

Others find it tough to name even one thing, saying:

"I don't know what it is, exactly. It just doesn't feel right. All I know is that I'm unhappy."

In order to find work that you love, it's important to take a closer look at what's NOT working, right now.

The more **specific** you can get about your frustrations, the better.

If you can't name any specifics, it's a good sign that it's **time for some soul-searching** ... and **self-reflection.**

Try this writing exercise to **clarify your frustrations** about your current work.

Write freely, and **try not to judge or censor** yourself.

Remember:

No one is going to read these words other than you.

Fill in the blanks (whichever ones apply to you and your work):

One thing that is definitely NOT okay about my current work is

_____

_____

_____

At work, it seriously annoys me when

_____

_____

_____

It bothers me when my boss / customers / clients

_____

_____

_____

I feel like I have the potential to

_____

_____

_____

but it's being wasted.

I'm so angry at my colleagues for

_____

_____

_____

I'm so angry at myself for

_____

_____

_____

I'm so sick over

_____

_____

_____

I'm so ashamed about

_____

_____

_____

I can't help blaming

_____

about

_____

_____

_____

I feel like I ought to have

_____

_____

by now.

I'm so jealous of people who

_____

_____

_____

I feel like I need to grieve the fact that

_____

_____

_____

Clarifying your desires and deal breakers.

When you're single and dating, hoping to find the love of your life, you may have certain "deal breakers."

If you want kids and they don't, that might be a deal breaker for you.

If you're seeking someone with an adventurous spirit who is willing to be your lifelong travel companion, and they hate flying with a seething passion, that might be a deal breaker for you.

It's ok to have deal breakers when it comes to your work, too.

Or, to put it another way:

It's ok to own your desires and preferences, and to give yourself permission to create a career that aligns with those desires and preferences, beautifully.

By clarifying some of your **biggest frustrations,** you've already taken a **big step** towards doing just that: finding work that is fully aligned with who you are.

Next?

We'll flip to the positive end of the spectrum, and explore what IS working.

STEP **3**

What IS Working?

Back when my professional work included actively practicing as an attorney (in the area of family law, mostly), I encountered a considerable amount of manipulation and game-playing.

I really disliked this negativity. But even on really tough days, I came back to the fact that helping clients made me so happy.

By focusing on that bright spot, I was eventually able to choose two other separate areas where I wanted to focus my career — life coaching and psychology — both of which offered me opportunities to do even MORE of what I loved.

That's why it's so valuable to **identify those little bright spots**, even if you're unhappy at work.

Those flickers of "silver lining" can serve as clues, pointing to the kind of work that you'll love so much more.

Use this next **writing exercise** to jot down some of the things about your current job or career that are

- Positive

- Uplifting

- Gratifying

And / or

- Meaningful

The things that make you **happy.**

As you write and reflect, look for patterns:

— What matters to you?

— What do you care about?

— What energizes you?

— Which qualities would you like to carry into whatever type of work you choose, next?

Fill in the blanks:

One thing that I really enjoy about my current job is

_____

_____

_____

_____

One thing I'll miss if I leave this job is

_____

_____

_____

_____

One project I'm proud of — and that I cared deeply about — was

_____

_____

_____

_____

One thing I wish I was asked to do more — because I really like it! — is

_____

_____

_____

_____

A story: From feeling miserable to feeling happy.

Here's a story about a client who was miserable at work, but then made a list of all the things that make her happy.

As she began to look for patterns and connect the dots, she found clues to illuminate a beautiful new career …

Becky came to see me because she wanted a career change. She was in a high paying job as a mental health professional with the potential to climb up the ladder — but she felt **worn-out** by her day-to-day work activities.

Here's a summary of how she described the predicament that she found herself in:

My position is impressive. But I'm bored. I feel like I'm at a dead-end. I want to do something much more thrilling and fulfilling.

Until now, Becky's search for new career options had left her **bewildered** and **overwhelmed**.

My husband tells me to download this career-finder app!

My friend says to create a website and blog!

My sister says to network and tell people I'm job hunting!

She also felt frustrated.

I just don't know what my passion is.

Becky was also **afraid** that if she committed to a new career, she might **miss out** on an even better opportunity.

I asked Becky to close her eyes, take a deep breath and relax.

Then, I suggested that she spend a few moments thinking about the last time she was:

- Totally happy ...

- Totally engrossed in doing something ...

- Totally focused.

Pretty soon her face lit up with a **lovely, contented glow.**

Clearly, **her thoughts were making her happy.**

When Becky opened her eyes, I gave her a pen and paper and asked her to list all of the times that she remembered enjoying doing something that made her happy, no matter how "random" or "off the wall" it might seem.

Becky loved:

— Taking her niece clothes-shopping

— Cooking for others (and sharing the recipes)

and

— Expressing her opinions about healthy living to anyone who would listen

Initially, she thought that the logical next step would be to pursue retail buying. But the thought of working in retail didn't excite her. It triggered a familiar feeling: **boredom**.

This taught Becky an important lesson:

— Just because she enjoys doing something **occasionally** (for recreation, or as a hobby) that doesn't mean it needs to become her "work."

And ...

— If emotions like "resentment" or "boredom" come into the mix, then it's a definite **thumbs down.**

In a follow-up visit, I encouraged Becky to review her list of things that made her happy and see if there were any dots to connect — any common threads that linked the items together.

She realized that above all, she loved:

— Sharing knowledge.

And

— She particularly loved sharing what she knew about:

- Clothes

- Cooking

And

- Healthy living

Any time she had an opportunity to **share** something wonderful with people who didn't know about it, she felt so **happy**.

Betty felt good about these realizations, but she knew that she didn't have all the pieces of the puzzle [yet!] to take the next step. That's why she wondered:

How is that going to lead me to the job that's right for me?

Then, serendipity struck.

A friend of hers who hosted his own talk radio show had to leave town for a family emergency. He needed someone to host his show that night. Becky agreed to fill in for him, to talk about healthy lifestyles.

During the first few moments of the show, she was really, really **nervous**. But then she **relaxed and began to feel so at home.**

Before long, she was flowing along. **She loved it!**

And so did the producer and the audience (the phones were ringing off the hook!)

After that, Becky became a regular guest on her friend's show, and was invited to be a guest on other radio shows as well. As one host told her:

You're a natural.

Becky is now looking into hosting her own healthy lifestyle radio show. She has several sponsors already lined up.

She's also teaching private cooking lessons for individuals and couples, where she helps clients develop tasty and healthy menus. She's loving this **fun, educational** experience — and it's **lucrative,** too!

And it all started by ...

Making a simple list of things that light up her heart.

Now that you've identified **your biggest frustrations** about your work, as well as a few **things that make you feel happy,** let's move onto our next step:

Exploring your options.

(I bet you've got far more than you think...)

STEP **4**

Seeing ALL the Options.

When you're in a job that you don't like, the first impulse for many people is …

To quit!

(Or to resign yourself to your "fate." Because …

— *It's "too hard" to change.*

Or

— *It's "too late".*)

Quitting is one option — and, it might ultimately be the right one.

But it's not always the ONLY option.

If feasible, you might also ...

— Apply for a different position inside your own company.

— Request a different kind of working arrangement — telecommuting from home, working four days a week, or switching to a morning shift.

— Ask for a raise.

— Ask for a sabbatical.

— Ask for different kinds of projects and challenges.

— Ask for appropriate forms of support (an intern, more guidance, more time to complete projects) so that you don't always feel so overwhelmed.

And even if quitting is ultimately the best choice, invariably there can STILL be lots of options.

If feasible, you might ...

— Find a similar job — but at a different company. Shift into a similar industry.

— Switch into a totally different industry.

— Go freelance as a contractor or consultant. Launch your own business — or a side-business.

Or,

— Some amazing combination of several options!

Expanding your mindset.

This step is all about creating the opportunity for you to get into an **expansive frame of mind** so that you can **see ALL of your options** before zeroing in and forming a plan.

Unleasing your creativity.

It's hard to think creatively (or plan effectively) when you're feeling burdened with **negative emotions.** So before launching into the next trio of exercises, take some time to **calm and center yourself** with a few deep breaths.

You might choose to:

- Go outside for a walk ...

- Lie down on the grass ...

- Rest under a tree ...

- Sit by a body of water

Or

- Go anywhere else that opens your mind and heart.

If you do some research on **the benefits of "travel"** — any form of travel, whether it's hopping on a plane or simply taking a new bicycle route to work — you'll find support for the fact that travel **stimulates creativity and promotes more effective thinking.**

Give yourself the gift of a "change of scenery."

It may unlock **creative solutions and career possibilities** you've never considered before.

Developing the mindset for visionary planning.

Once you're

— **Feeling calmer**

And you've

— Settled yourself in a location that feels **inspiring**

Then,

Try these next three exercises to

— **Prime your mind for visionary planning.**

Exercise 1: An emotional inventory.

Take stock of how you feel about having to make a job or career change.

If you relate to any of the feelings below, complete the sentences that apply to you.

I'm angry because

_____

_____

_____

I'm frustrated because

_____

_____

_____

I'm sad because

_____

_____

_____

I'm afraid because

_____

_____

_____

Releasing your emotions

If you filled in any blanks, then set aside 5 to 10 minutes for yourself in a private place, sometime today.

Be sure that you won't be interrupted, so that you can give this exercise your undivided attention.

Pillow exercise

— Take a pillow and gently hold it up to your face.

Be aware of what you're feeling (example: anger, frustration or fear).

— Release your feelings by screaming into the pillow (it muffles the sound).

If you're sad, it's ok to cry and feel your loss.

— By releasing your emotions **safely**, you're **releasing** some **emotional "weight"** that can make it harder to see options clearly, choose wisely and move forward

Exercise No. 2: Breathe into possibility.

In a quiet, private place, close your eyes.

Breathe in slowly to the count of 2.

Hold your breath to the count of 2.

Release your breath slowly to the count of 2.

Repeat this exercise a few more times.

Then,

Picture yourself taking action to change your work situation — from one that you hate, into one that you **love**.

Picture yourself in your new job or career ...

— Happy

— Rewarded

— Satisfied on so many levels.

Notice:

— What you are wearing

— Where you are working

Picture your environment:

— What does it smell like?

— What does it feel like?

— What does it look like, around you?

Take in all the sensory details.

Feel how amazing it feels ... to have found work that you love.

Take a few more deep breaths, breathing into that scene. **Breathing into what's possible.**

Now open your eyes.

Pause for a moment —

So you can write notes about what you saw in your visualization.

There are **gems in the teeniest details** of these kinds of visualization activities.

It's a good idea to **jot down** as much of what you saw / felt / heard as you can.

Otherwise, **it's easy to forget** those **tiny details** later and the **insights** they were offering.

Next:

Tying this all together, with **a letter**.

Read the following letter out loud, as if you were reading the words to your very best friend in the whole world:

"Dear {Your Name},

I know that you're unhappy at work. But you won't feel this way forever.

You are already working towards a more meaningful job or career. And here's what I want to remind you:

Trust yourself.

Trust that you'll find **one little bright spot of happiness** *in your current work — or at least, find a way to tolerate it — as you build something better.*

Trust **your ideas.**

Trust **your strengths.**

Trust that **you can set goals for yourself and deliver results.**

Trust that you can take **calculated, appropriate risks.**

Trust **in the process,** *knowing that this journey may take longer than you'd like, and may take a lot more effort than you'd expect.*

You can be proud of every little step.

Trust and **remember** *that millions of people have found work that they love.*

Trust that **it's possible for you, too.**

Exercise No. 3: Yes, and!

In improv comedy, there's a technique known as "Yes, and!"

"Kevin, you're late again!"

"Yes, and ... I have a confession to make. I'm a werewolf."

"Well, that explains all the fur clogging the drains..."

The "Yes, and!" technique is a way of building **possibilities on top of possibilities, without getting overly attached** to your initial idea.

This leads to hilarious scenes that are often even funnier than one comedian could possibly conceive of, alone. Scenes that veer off in **unexpected and exciting directions.**

You can use this same technique to generate **new career possibilities** for yourself — just like an improv comedian building a scene ...

Read these examples and then fill in the blanks:

*I can find **work that I love**.*

*Yes, and ... I can find at least one reason to **appreciate and enjoy my current work, in the meantime!***

*Yes, and ... I can **take baby steps every day,** building towards a bigger goal!*

*Yes, and ... I can hold myself and my colleagues to higher standards, **taking pride** in my work!*

Yes, and ... I can

_____

_____

_____

Yes, and ... I can

_____

_____

_____

Yes, and ... I can

_____

_____

_____

Yes, and ... I can

_____

_____

_____

Yes, and ... I can

_____

_____

_____

Yes, and ... I can

_____

_____

_____

Now that you've shifted into a more expansive frame of mind, let's get into specifics.

What's your dream — and where do you see yourself in two years?

STEP **5**

What's Your Dream?

The philosopher and linguist Ludwig Wittgenstein once said:

"That which cannot be said, cannot be thought."

Meaning:

If you can't describe something in words — either out loud, or in writing — it doesn't really exist as a fully-formed thought, yet.

That's why **writing down your goals, intentions and dreams** is so powerful.

In verbally expressing your dreams using the written word, they become **clearer**. They start to become **real**.

Here's a writing exercise to help write a story about your life ... in two years.

Fill in the blanks with an open mind and heart, without being concerned about how you're going to get there, just yet.

This is YOUR dream life.

YOUR dream work.

YOUR dream story!

Dream **big or small.**

It doesn't matter.

Your only task is to **stay true to what you really desire.**

In two years, I will ...

Be living in

_____

_____

_____

Wake up to the sounds of

_____
_____
_____

Enjoy a lovely breakfast of

_____
_____
_____

Get dressed for work by putting on

_____
_____
_____

Travel to work by

_____
_____
_____

Work at a place that feels like

_____

_____

_____

Be surrounded by colleagues / collaborators / clients / customers who

_____

_____

_____

Have a boss (or mentor) who

_____

_____

_____

Spend my days

_____

_____

_____

Spend my evenings

_____

_____

_____

Spend my free time

_____

_____

_____

Be appreciated for the way that I

_____

_____

_____

Be rewarded for my good work with

_____

_____

_____

Be regarded as someone who

_____

_____

_____

Honor my aspiration in life by

_____

_____

_____

Writing down your dream — your future story — is SO powerful.

But sometimes, when you're feeling burnt out or disgruntled about your current job or career, it can be hard to get into that **"visionary" frame of mind.**

If it feels difficult (or even impossible) to dream up a new future right now, **take baby steps.**

Start by continuing to **notice little things** about your current life that **you DO enjoy.**

Things that **DO make you happy.**

Things that **you want MORE** of, in the future.

Here's **a true story** about how I made the transition into my current life and career — living in beautiful Hawaii, working in the field of emotional health.

I didn't have perfect clarity about the work I was meant to be doing, at the beginning.

It took time to figure it out, but it all started when I began simply noticing little things that I liked and desired ...

After I graduated from high school in South Africa, I attended college in New York City. I lived in a suburb outside of the city, which meant each day's commute was (roughly) a 90-minute train ride, round trip. That was a lot of commuting ... and a lot of time to be chatting with other commuters.

But it was a great gift.

Because of that experience, I realized how much I enjoyed talking to people, listening, and asking questions ... and how easy and natural that felt for me, especially with someone I'd never met before.

And I remember during one commute, thinking to myself:

"I really enjoy this. I want to do something with my life where I **talk** *to people, and* **listen**, *and* **offer helpful insight**.*"*

Around that time, I saw snow for the first time. That was also the first time I'd experienced bitterly cold winters. And wearing layers upon layers of clothes to shield myself from the extreme cold weather (along with statically-charged hair, chapped lips, and watery eyes). But then, once inside, having to quickly shed the layers — because it was too hot.

So as I commuted in overheated trains, gazing at the merciless weather outside, I thought:

*"I want to live in a place where I can wear **short sleeves** all-the-time."*

Fast forward to now.

*As I sit here writing this life guide, I have just finished doing a life coaching session in my office in Hawaii — **talking, listening,** and **offering helpful insight.***

*Guess what I'm wearing? My favorite **short sleeved** blouse (plus a skirt!).*

It took a while, but I did manifest my dream.

STEP **6**

Make a Plan

Walt Disney once said:

"All our dreams can come true, if we have the courage to pursue them."

And Mr. Disney was a man who knew a thing or two about taking "impossible" dreams + fantasies, and making them a reality!

He's quite right, though. Whatever dream you have for your life and your work ... IS possible.

If you find yourself having thoughts like:

"Oh, sure, it's possible for OTHER people to find meaningful work (or make changes) ... but they're not dealing with the same limitations or circumstances as ME."

Or:

"It's just too late for me. I've made my bed, now I have to lie in it, whether it's comfortable or not!"

Or:

"I literally can't afford to leave my current line of work. I have people depending on me."

Or, if you're thinking any other variations of

"I can't."

Here are three pieces I highly encourage you to read. They're all published online, and they're all authored by me.

"Why Positive Affirmations Don't Always Work (And What Does)."
— From Tiny Buddha.

http://tinybuddha.com/blog/why-positive-affirmations-dont-always-work-and-what-does/

"Just Believe." How I Learned to Trust in the Universe, Even When All Hope Seemed Lost.
— From Positively Positive.

http://www.positivelypositive.com/2015/03/26/just-believe-how-i-learned-to-trust-in-the-universe-even-when-all-hope-seemed-lost/

20 Career-Boosting Steps You Can Take Before New Year's Eve
— From my column, Be Well at Work, over at The Muse: an amazing website for career and business advice.

https://www.themuse.com/advice/20-careerboosting-steps-you-can-take-before-new-years-eve?ref=carousel-slide-0

Feeling inspired? Excellent!

Now — holding that dream you wrote down in Step 5 — it's time to figure out **your first three baby steps.**

(Those first few steps are often the toughest).

Don't overthink these steps.

You probably already know — perfectly well — what you need to do, to get started.

Your first step might be as simple as

"Set aside 1 hour a week for personal reflection and career research at the library."

Or

"Set up a coffee date with Sally, and pick her brain about how she got started as a professional organizer."

Keep it simple.

Set the bar lower than you think you ought to — so that you'll actually **complete the steps, building some confidence and momentum** as you go!

In order to make my dream come true, I need to:

1. _____

_____

_____

2. _____

_____

_____

3. _____

_____

_____

Don't plan any further than those first three steps.

You don't need to, right now.

Once you've completed them, then you can plot out the next three steps.

When you're feeling **overwhelmed**, just check in with yourself and ask:

"What is the very next step?"

Place your focus there. One foot in front of the other.

And eventually, with **devotion and patience**?

You WILL build your dream.

When it just feels like "too much" ...

If you find yourself feeling overwhelmed, apprehensive, or unable to take the action that you want to, that might mean that something is stopping you from moving forward.

If that feels like you — like you're being blocked by a boulder you can't quite see — you may want to consult a qualified counseling professional or possibly partner with a coach.

STEP 7

Keep Working ... For Love.

I've said it before, and I'll say it again:

When you LOVE your work, you DO better work.

And the whole world benefits from your love.

You might not be blissfully engaged in work that you love tomorrow, or one week from today, or even a year from today.

It takes time to build a dream.

To change course, mid-stream.

This is a long game. Patience is essential.

In order to go the distance, **taking care of yourself** and **being kind to yourself** is essential — even if you're a long, long way away from your ideal career.

Here's a writing exercise to remind yourself WHY you're on this journey — especially in those moments when you feel like quitting.

Fill in the blanks:

I'm committed to finding work that I love because

_____

_____

_____

I am willing to be patient because

_____

_____

_____

I'll probably feel scared, at times, but I trust that

_____

_____

_____

The BEST part about my life right now is

_____

_____

_____

The BEST part about my career right now is

_____

_____

_____

I'm SO excited to start moving closer towards

_____

_____

_____

Remember:

In order to build your dream career, you must treat yourself with self-respect and care.

You can't "hate" or "punish" yourself into finding work that you love.

Love always begins ... **with love.**

A FEW FINAL WORDS

When you decide to change your work — or any part of your life — it's like **building a bridge** from your **current reality** into **a new and better world**.

You can build that bridge with:

- Anger, shame and blame.

Or you can build it with:

- Joy, hope, kindness to yourself and others.

Either way, that bridge is getting built.

Either way, you're going to cross over to the other side.

It's up to you to decide how that crossing is going to feel.

It's your life, so ... **make it feel good.**

MORE TIPS, MORE TOOLS

3 FAQs: Work /Career Challenges With a Fresh, Uplifting Spin

Ready for even more tips and tools to boost the strengths that you can naturally bring to any job, career or business venture?

Read on for my answers to some of the more typical questions that clients who wanted to change (and / or improve how they handled) their careers or jobs, have asked. (Q & As have been summarized / paraphrased for privacy, and to maximize learning).

And get your pencil and paper ready for fill-in-the-blank writing exercises and worksheets.

Enjoy!

Question No. 1 — Dragging my feet

Overcoming fear of failure

I've been wanting to start my own business and venture out on my own for some time. I have a job, but I'm not challenged and there are personnel issues that really get to me.

But despite my good intentions to get going with my own business, I just don't seem to make headway. I start lots of projects related to getting the business off the ground, but I rarely finish them. In this regard, I find myself thinking, too often:

"Why do I put off until tomorrow what I should have done yesterday?"

And since it's the end of the year right now, and I'm thinking about New Year's resolutions for my own business, I wish I could stop seeing the same resolutions on my New Year's list, year after year.

I don't consider myself a lazy person, but I'm starting to think that maybe I am just lazy, when it comes to "doing my own thing" business-wise.

Can you help me to understand why I'm dragging my feet?

Response:

Sounds like you're wrestling with procrastination. This is a troublesome habit that can cause major problems, depending on how severe the habit is.

Generally speaking though, **procrastinators aren't inherently lazy.** More often than not, they develop this **self-defeating habit** in response to **something they experienced while growing up.**

In other words, if you reflect upon your habit and become a little introspective about it, you might find, as have many other procrastinators, that:

The procrastination habit has its roots, in one way or another, in how you were raised.

Example:

Here's some insight that one client gained, after we addressed his procrastination habit:

I see now that my procrastination is a reaction to the fact that my parents were so controlling that during childhood I never experienced any independence (age-appropriate, of course) or learned any self-discipline that I now understand was necessary to accomplish goals.

That's why, as an adult, I've been so defiant and spent many years rebelling against rules and regulations — like due dates and deadlines. No wonder that I'm always running into jams like incurring late payment fees or missing a deadline to buy concert tickets.

Good news!

Procrastination, like any habit, can be unlearned.

That's exactly what this client did.

Once he began to "connect the dots" as to where and why this habit manifested — and to resolve any feelings (anger, grief) that he had about this problem behavior — he was able to replace the "dragging his feet" habit with a **new habit**. A habit that enabled him to **accomplish his goals**, with **ease** and with **satisfaction**.

Here's another reason why people have a hard time getting into gear and taking action:

People who procrastinate also tend to be responding to some type of fear within themselves.

This fear can cause them to **avoid doing what needs to be done**.

Follow-up question no. 1

I think I just had a "lightbulb moment" as I was listening to you speak about procrastination.

This is not about starting my own business though... but when my 11-year-old son asks me for help with his homework, I feel hesitant and like I'd rather not get involved — even though I want to help my son and I'm capable of helping him with his homework.

My "lightbulb moment?"

As was growing up, my parents were always finding fault with what I did. They were constantly criticizing me for never doing anything right.

At the time, I didn't think of it in these terms, but I definitely felt like a complete failure, in their eyes.

So, could that be why I hesitate to help my child with homework? Could it be that I'm afraid I'll mess up because that's what I was criticized for during childhood.

Am I on the right track with my insight from this "lightbulb moment?"

Response:

That certainly sounds like a plausible reason for your reluctance to help your son with his homework. Fear of failure.

Parents who were criticized during their childhood, often become procrastinators — both as a parent and as a person.

On a subconscious level, the fear of failure "script" that's operating, tends to sound something like this:

I can't {insert task} because if I mess up, then I'm a failure as a parent and as a person, just like I felt when I was a child. I don't want to fail. I'm afraid I will. So I can't {insert task}.

You can see why this fear would result in procrastination.

In your particular example with your child's homework, the fear of failure "script" that's operating on a subconscious level, may very well sound something like this:

I can't help my child with his homework because if I mess up then I'm a failure as a parent and as a person, just like I felt when I was a child. I don't want to fail. I'm afraid I will. So I can't help my child with his homework.

So, yes, your "lightbulb moment" offered you an extremely valuable insight into why you were encountering resistance to helping your child.

This resistance is also probably a contributing factor to your resistance to actualize your goals with building your own business.

Now that you are aware of this, and if you choose to safely release any feelings (anger, grief) that you may have about how this habit has held you back [see Step 4, Exercise 1, "Pillow exercise"], you may very well find that you feel a lot closer to being able to achieve your goals with setting up your own business.

Follow-up question no. 2

I'm also a perfectionist. So it takes me forever to finish doing something that I need to do, like writing an email to my son's teacher.

That could easily take say, 15 minutes to do ... but for me it takes much longer because I'm refining it, and then refining it again, and in the end, I'm still not satisfied and find things wrong with it.

A lot of the time I never finish what I'm doing because I run out of time to keep fiddling with it until it's "just right" — which it never is.

Is this "never satisfied" outlook that I have part of the same procrastination habit / problem?

Response:

It's not surprising that you also wrestle with perfectionism.

Many procrastinators who fear failure are also perfectionists.

Example:

Years ago, I worked with a client who was a licensed practical nurse. At the time, she wanted to become a registered nurse and advance her career. To achieve this goal, she was attending nursing school.

She came to see me because day in and day out, during every class, and whenever she did homework, here's what went through her mind:

I must get straight "A's," otherwise I'm a failure.

This meant that when she was faced with a writing assignment, she expected herself to become an **expert on the topic** before she began her writing.

The result?

This made her **anxious** and caused her to procrastinate.

How?

When she would sit down at the computer to type her paper, instead of doing just that, **she would distract herself** by checking her e-mail, again and again.

This is essentially what she said about prioritizing checking her email rather than typing her paper:

I feel guilty for this, but at least I don't have to face the sense of failure I feel when I write.

As far as I'm concerned, my work is just never good enough to submit.

Here's what happened next:

Her **procrastination had caused her career to suffer** because by that time, had she not been wrestling with procrastination, she would already graduated and increased her earning power.

Instead, at the time she first came to see me, she facing two major problems because of her procrastination:

1. She was having to repeat classes.

2. She was facing the possibility that she might not graduate.

That's why, when I first responded to your initial question, I identified procrastination as *"a troublesome habit that can cause major problems, depending on how severe the habit is."*

Happy ending no. 1

Fortunately, after several meetings, my client was able to get on the right track and not allow fear of failure to hold her back any more.

It took a while, but **she did end up graduating.** Consequently, she was thrilled that **she achieved her goal of advancing in her career.**

And just like this determined individual **achieved her goal** by resolving her fears, so can other procrastinators, including you — starting your own business may be closer to becoming a reality than you think!

Happy ending no. 2

In time, this dad resolved his fears that were prompting his procrastination. Then he was able to achieve two of his most important goals, with ease:

1. He was able to confidently help his son with homework.

2. He also became a proud small business owner.

Impact of procrastination on children

During this dad's final meeting with me, although he was so pleased with his progress, and the fact that he had achieved his goals, he asked, with concern:

Now that I see how my upbringing contributed to me being a procrastinator, is my son going to be a procrastinator because I was?

Sometimes he drags his feet to get things done (like doing his chores), but I just thought that was something he'd grow out of.

Should I be concerned?

Response:

Typically, children tend to emulate behaviors that they observe in their parents / caregivers.

Meaning: If their mom or dad procrastinates, they tend to do the same, or some variation of that.

Example:

One mom who came to see me about her own procrastination issues, was concerned that her 9-year-old son might have picked up this behavior from her.

Why?

Her son was **avoiding** doing his homework, **putting it off** until the last minute.

This is not unlike this mom's own behavior, as she described it:

*I have a hard time finding the impetus to start — and finish — things that I need to do. It's like **I'm not motivated**.*

Here's what she tells herself when she is faced with starting or finishing a task:

This isn't important.

Or

I work better under pressure.

Like many procrastinators who **wait till the last minute** to do something, this mom likes the **adrenalin rush** that she gets when she's "backed-up-against-the-wall" so to speak.

So, it wouldn't be all that surprising (although not inevitable), that her son puts off doing his homework (and most likely, puts off doing other tasks, as well).

This child, and others who are raised with role-models who engage in similar procrastination-type behavior, could be at risk for **developing into adults who set goals,** but then **sabotage their own efforts** to achieve these goals.

How?

By **delaying** taking any action to get things done.

Stop the habit, early

As for your son dragging his feet to do what needs to be done, it's best to **nip this behavior in the bud**.

This way, he can develop **self-discipline** that can equip him to get things done, rather than dragging his feet.

Positive change in a parent's behavior = Positive change in a child's behavior

You might also notice that as your son sees a change in your behavior (no more procrastination), as is typical with children, he will emulate what he sees, and get his chores done on time.

That said, it's possible that he made need some professional assistance to resolve any procrastination behavior that he may have adopted by observing you.

Alternatively, you may need some professional assistance to learn **parenting skills** to help your son refrain from any procrastination behavior.

Either way, I suggest that you take a look at a life guide that I wrote for parents.

It's called: <u>**How To Get Your Kids To Cooperate: And Help Them Become the BEST Grown-Ups They Can Be.**</u>

<u>https://amzn.to/2V4AzxD</u>

Inside this life guide you'll find the basics of positive discipline — including tools and practices that you can use **right away.**

Question No. 2 — Delays, avoidance, inaction

Overcoming fear of success

I've been ready to change jobs for a while. I know what I want to do next, career-wise, and I've been working at a feverish pace to get all my ducks lined up to make the career-move possible.

Until recently, I've been super excited about this potential change, and I believe I will be successful at my new venture. There will be a guaranteed increase in income and professional status.

Everything is set up for me to take the next step, and go for my final interview. This is a routine step, rather than being decisive as to whether I get the job or not. The deal is done. I've been told that once I do this interview, I'm "in!".

But during the past month, I've found myself stuck... dead in my tracks ...

I give myself every excuse in the book to delay ... and avoid taking this final step.

So nothing's happening.

I'm afraid I'll blow this incredibly opportunity (my dream job) if I don't act soon.

Why have I not been able to take this final step? Why am I stuck?

Hoping you can shed some light on this.

[Note to reader:

After hearing the client's question along with the background information leading up to the question, as summarized on the preceding page, I found that before I could respond fully, I would need more details from the client.

I then asked the client some additional questions so that I could learn more information from him, and about the challenge he was dealing with.

Once I received that information, I formulated the response that you will see below.

I have not included a summary of my follow-up questions to the client or his answers, since it is not necessary for an understanding of my response.]

Response:

This may seem **counterintuitive** because it's clear that, from an intellectual standpoint, you really want to make this career move.

Meaning: **Intellectually**, you're able to wrap your mind around moving forward as planned. But…

Something is stopping you, dead in your tracks.

That "something" appears to be **fear**. Specifically,

Fear of success

This might sound counter-intuitive. Like:

I want to be successful, why would I be afraid of what I want?

That's because sometimes our **intellect** (I want to be successful) and our **emotions** (I'm afraid of success) are **at odds**.

Put another way:

Our **conscious** mind desires one thing (success), but somewhere in our **subconscious**, there is a fear of that same thing (fear of success). Hence the conscious and subconscious are **at odds**.

That said, your fear (worry) appears to be at least two-fold. You're worried that if you become successful:

1. Your siblings [who work in the same field] and colleagues might become **jealous and resentful** of you.

2. Other people (e.g., parents, employers) would have **high expectations** of you.

   *(Then I'd feel **pressured**, especially since I already have high standards for myself.)*

Another reason that many people who **want** professional success, but at the same time **fear** that potential success, is because they fear that if go "all out" and "reach for the stars," professionally, they might turn into a **workaholic**.

Here's how one person put it:

I procrastinate compulsively. So if I aim for success, I'll probably be compulsive about being productive, too.

Follow-up question

Your response rings true with me - even the third reason applies to me, actually.

Honestly, I'm feeling a bit frustrated and somewhat hopeless about my fears, at the moment. Like,

"Why can't I make a career change that brings me success, like others do and have done?"

Response:

Rest assured, many people have overcome this habit and taken charge of their lives.

You've taken an important step by reaching out and sharing your challenge with procrastination.

Next step: For homework, I'm going to give you a form that contains a **writing exercise** for you to complete.

This exercise involves trying to identify and **write down each situation that triggers your procrastination.**

Then ask yourself:

"Why do I procrastinate? What am I afraid of?"

Even though I've given you a jump-start on this (by identifying three possible reasons for your procrastination), the answers that you come up with can help you further understand your fears.

Example:

Another client I worked with, resisted submitting job applications — even though this would mean a promotion which was something she deeply desired.

After completing the writing exercise, she realized that she was dreading the fact that her applications might be rejected. As she put it:

I've always taken rejection personally.

I remember how bad I felt as a kid when I wasn't picked for the basketball team or to act in a school play. On top of that, my parents would also get mad when I wasn't picked.

*Seems like I'm still **afraid of feeling rejected** if I don't get a job that I want.*

In this instance, I commended this client for her insight. I then encouraged her to **put her fears to rest**, saying:

You can now see, those fears have nothing to do with your efforts to find a job.

Now, back to the client above, who was resisting going for a final job interview.

After completing the writing exercise, he came to **even more insights** as to why he was feeling paralyzed (figuratively speaking) when faced with moving forward with the job interview.

Example:

He realized that another reason he had been avoiding the job interview was because he would lapse into **doubt**, afraid that perhaps he was "biting off more than he could chew."

For homework, I assigned him another writing exercise to:

- **Strengthen his confidence**

and, in doing so,

- **Diffuse his doubt**

The exercise involved **writing down three affirmations** that he would read out loud to himself, daily.

Example:

I can handle the requirements of this new job with poise, grace and professionalism.

I deserve to be in this new position.

After doing a few more homework exercises, following his sessions with me, this client felt ready to go for the interview.

Happy Ending.

At a follow-up session, he reported that he had:

- **Completed** the interview with flying colors

- Been officially **hired** for the new job

Pleased, excited and appreciative of how helpful our work had been to him, he said:

I'm feeling so much better. I feel confident — instead of that self-defeating dread — about starting my new job, next week.

How about you? Is procrastination holding you back?

Are you feeling stuck because of a fear of:

— Failure?

— Success?

— Something else {insert word}?

Would you like to **try the two writing exercises** that were so helpful to this client?

You can find the templates for these exercises coming up on the next few pages.

I hope they're useful!

Start Here, With This First Writing Exercise To Understand Your Fears.

Identify and **write down each situation that triggers your procrastination.** Use additional space, if you need it.

I drag my feet when

_____

_____

_____

I distract myself instead of doing

_____

_____

_____

I avoid doing

_____

_____

_____

I delay doing

_____

_____

_____

I postpone doing

_____

_____

_____

I put off doing

_____

_____

_____

I dread doing

_____

_____

_____

Next:

For each situation that you identified as a trigger for your procrastination, **ask yourself:**

"Why do I procrastinate? What am I afraid of?"

Then, **fill in the blanks** in the pages that follow with your written answers.

Try not to:

- Overthink

- Edit what you write

- Pay attention to spelling, grammar

- Overanalyze the topic you're writing about

- Censor what you write

or to

- Have expectations as to what your answers should be

Just **relax** and **let your words flow**.

There are big costs to procrastination. Understanding your fears is key to resolving this self-sabotaging habit.

If necessary, use additional space to write down your thoughts.

"Why do I procrastinate? What am I afraid of?"

_____

_____

_____

"Why do I procrastinate? What am I afraid of?"

_____

_____

_____

"Why do I procrastinate? What am I afraid of?"

_____

_____

_____

"Why do I procrastinate? What am I afraid of?"

_____

_____

_____

"Why do I procrastinate? What am I afraid of?"

_____

_____

_____

"Why do I procrastinate? What am I afraid of?"

_____

_____

_____

"Why do I procrastinate? What am I afraid of?"

_____

_____

_____

"Why do I procrastinate? What am I afraid of?"

_____

_____

_____

Fill in the Blanks in This Second Writing Exercise, and Start To Build Confidence ...

Specifically:

— Starting today ...

Write Down Three Affirmations.

Example:

I am confident that I can do a terrific job with the new business I want to build.

I am talented and I create a great product.

I am ready for this new responsibility.

— Then . . .

For the **next seven days**

Read These Affirmations Out Loud to Yourself, Daily.

Repeat this cycle for two more weeks.

This means:

— On the first day of week number two ...

Write Down Three New Affirmations.

For the **next 7 days of week number two**

Read These Affirmations Out Loud to Yourself, Daily.

— Then . . .

— On the first day of week number three . . .

Write Down Three New Affirmations.

For the **next 7 days of week number three**

Read These Affirmations Out Loud to Yourself, Daily.

Question No. 3 — Communication

Handling Poor Communicators Effectively

I'm looking for a new job. I have put some feelers out, I have good connections, and I'm hopeful that something will work out. There's one thing that I'm dreading though...

All the jobs that I've worked at so far, have had bosses and / or managers who were poor communicators. Sometimes, this caused confusion like after I completed a particular project in the manner that I thought it needed to be done, then my manager said it was supposed to be done differently.

I'm dreading running into this type of poor communication in my next job.

I don't like confrontation, actually it scares me. So when there's confusion, like when the manager said that the project I completed was not done in the manner that he wanted, I don't feel comfortable saying something like:

"You never told me that you wanted it this way."

To be quite honest, I don't like speaking up, period. I have good ideas and I'm good at what I do, but when I need to speak up at work, I often freeze and sometimes get "tongue-tied".

I'd prefer that the bosses / managers communicated clearly. So that I wouldn't have to "guess" what they want, misinterpret their "directions", or have to sort things out with them, after the fact.

How can I handle these communication issues more comfortably?

Response:

Thank you for your detailed question. It's one that I believe a lot of people can relate to.

Why?

Because "speaking up" is something that so many people fear. Do you know what causes people to **freeze** and **get "tongue-tied"**, just like you describe in your question?

Fear

This means that your question invites a two-pronged response. In other words, there are two aspects that need to be addressed:

1. How to open up the lines of **communication** with bosses, managers, and others who are "lacking" when it comes to communication skills.

2. How to resolve **fears** about speaking up.

How To Get What You Need From Terrible Communicators

Regarding dealing with people who clearly need to brush up on their communication skills I strongly suggest that you read the article that I wrote on this topic. It's called:

3 Ways to Get What You Need From Terrible Communicators.

https://muse.cm/2JgeuKl

This article was originally published on my column, "Be Well At Work," which can be found on The Muse.[1] This article was also published online in TIME.

In the article, I discuss **how to ask for clarification** and I outline a script that you can individualize for your own use. Also included is an example of an actual script.

Next, I address something what commonly occurs when asking a poor communicator for clarification:

The response / clarification doesn't make any sense.

I offer **a script to help straighten out the unclear response.**

Finally, I address **what to do if poor communication continues** to be an issue.

How To Get Resolve Those Gut-Wrenching Fears About Speaking Up

As I said earlier, this type of fear is all-too-common. So much so, that some time ago I devised **a five-step process** that can be a good start to resolve some of those dreaded fears.

Not a week goes by where I don't encourage at least one client to utilize this process, in my office.

Fear is an emotion. It is possible to release this emotion (safely). And to resolve it.

---

[1] The Muse is an online platform that attracts more than 75 million people each year, to help them be at the top of their game at work.

Clients really appreciate this five-step process. Because it's effective. Because it works.

Here is an outline of the five steps.

Step 1. Accept How You Feel.

In order to begin to resolve your fear, it's necessary to let it be **OK that you are feeling afraid**.

It may seem like I'm stating the obvious, but so many people feel **ashamed or embarrassed** about being fearful.

Then they **judge / criticize** themselves for feeling this way.

Examples:

— *What's wrong with me, why am I acting like such a baby!*

— *I'm an adult, I shouldn't be feeling like such a scaredy cat.*

— *I'm tough... how embarrassing that I'm such a weakling!*

— *There's no reason to be scared. I'm not a baby.*

— *Oh grow up, you coward!*

— *When am I going to learn to act my age?*

— *Quit being so dramatic, there's nothing to be afraid of!*

— *I'm so embarrassed, I hope no one can tell how scared I am.*

As Long as This Internal Conflict Is Present

Between:

- **What We Actually Feel (Afraid)**

And:

- **How We Think We Should Feel (Unafraid)**

We Will Be Caught Up in This Conflict.

As long as this conflict is present we won't be able to focus on releasing and healing our fear.

This is why it's so important to diffuse this conflict with **self-acceptance**.

Then we'll be ready to move on to Step 2.

Step 2. Scream Out Your Fear.

That's right. Scream. Just like children do when they're afraid. They don't typically sit quietly and pretend to be happy.

Instead, they start screaming (typically to get an adult's attention and hopefully get their needs met). We can learn a lot from little kids and how they naturally express their feelings. And they get relief, too. Then, free from their fear, they feel calmer, more content, and happier. And you can too.

Here's the jist of what I say to clients when I'm encouraging / teaching them to release their fear, safely:

- For this exercise set aside some time (3 to 5 minutes).

- Make sure you won't be interrupted during this time.

- Find a quite space where you will have privacy.

- Grab a soft pillow

- Gently hold the pillow up to your face (it muffles sound).

- Visualize / imagine what you're afraid off.

- Allow yourself to feel the fear.

- Then scream out the fear (like a child does) into the pillow.

- Keep screaming until you feel some relief… a sense of calm.

Then, when you're ready, lower the pillow to your lap.

Take a deep breath in. Hold to the count of 1-2-3.

Exhale to the count of 1-2-3.

Repeat (Inhale to the count of 3, Exhale to the count of three).

Stand up, stretch, shake your hands and arms.

Relax.

Step 3. Be Sure to Scream Out Your Fear.

Yes, it's necessary to revisit Step 2 here, because it's so important.

Yet people have been tempted to skip this step. They think it's silly. They think it won't work.

It does work. And it has worked for those who've implemented it.

What hasn't worked, is trying to talk ourselves out of our fear… to minimize it… to somehow rationalize it away.

That's not solving the issue at all.

Why?

Because **fear is an emotion**. It can't be "explained" away, or "rationalized" away.

Why not?

Because for **healing** to occur, **emotional energy must be released** via safe expression, **not just talked about** via one's intellect.

So consider giving this scream-into-the-pillow tool a try. Think of it this way:

— It doesn't cost anything

And …

— You don't have to go anywhere (unlike having to make a trip to the gym, if you want to work out with weights, for example.) Your **emotional workout** can be done right in your own home.

Step 4. Comfort Your Inner Child.

After you've safely released some fear, and you're feeling calmer, it's time to take a look at **the source** of your fear.

Typically that leads us back to our **inner child** — that's the child who we once were, who (metaphorically-speaking) "lives on" within us, and expresses itself to us, via our emotions.

In this instance, the inner child would be the part of us that's harboring fear.

Why is that so?

Because, in this instance, that **inner child** might be a

— 5-year-old who was made fun of for how she recited a poem.

— 6-year-old who was criticized for how he pronounced certain words.

— 7-year-old who was mocked when raising his hand in class and giving a wrong answer.

These traumatic types of situations can cause a child to grow up into an adult who fears speaking up.

This Is Why It Is So Important To Nurture the Child That We Once Were, Who, in This Instance, Lives on Inside Us — Afraid.

Sometimes it takes consulting with a professional in order to heal and nurture the child within, and to understand why we feel the way we do. If you feel drawn to consult with a professional, it's wise to listen to that impulse and follow through.

That said, in order to heal our fear, it's not always necessary to know, down to the finest detail, why the child from our past, developed fears. Here are two **simple exercises** can help to **soothe fear**, and gently **strengthen confidence.** Try them if you'd like.

Each exercise takes about a minute or two, at the most. Since the exercises involve saying things out loud, make sure that when you do them you have:

- Privacy

And

- A few moments where you won't be interrupted, distracted or disturbed.

Exercise no. 1

Using a firm, but loving voice, say to yourself, out loud:

That was then, this is now. I am now longer that scared little child.

Exercise no. 2

Grab a soft pillow.

Wrap your arms around the pillow, as if you're hugging it.

While you're doing this, you can pretend or imagine that you're hugging the child that you once were.

Then say out loud:

I love you. I'm here for you. I won't abandon you.

I believe in you. I have confidence in you.

If it feels right, you can repeat these sentences for a second time.

This **soothing self-talk** can comfort the part of you that is still a small, scared child.

Once the child within you feels **safe and secure**, then fear can be a non-issue. Which means that fear of speaking up can be a non-issue.

You might be tempted to skip these exercises, and go onto Step 5.

Why?

Because the thought of saying these scripts out loud might seem odd or weird, or even childish.

That's understandable, many people feel that way about these types of exercises. But here's something you might want to ask yourself:

What have I got to lose by trying these exercises?

Does your answer sound like the one below?

Nothing, except fear of speaking up.

If yes, then...

You know what to do next!

Step 5. Acknowledge Your Right To Speak.

Recap:

So far you have:

- Accepted your fear (Step 1)

- Released some of it safely (Step 2)

- Made sure that you released some of it (Step 3)

And

- Soothed your scared, inner child (Step 4).

Now, it's time to focus on speaking up.

It's Time To Remind Yourself That You Have Every Right To Speak Up at Work.

To do this, it can be helpful to ask yourself two simple, but powerful, questions. It's best to answer these questions in writing. To do this, try the writing exercise that follows.

Even though there are only two questions, take your time to formulate your answers. Don't rush. Let your answers reflect your deepest thoughts.

At the same time, try not to overthink. Write from your heart. Write from your gut.

Fill in the Blanks in This Writing Exercise, and Reflect on These Two Questions ...

Question no. 1

Who am I?

_____

_____

_____

Sample answer:

I have an important function in this company.

I am competent and I do my job very well.

Question no. 2

What am I doing here [as I'm about to speak up to my boss]?

_____

_____

_____

Sample answer:

I am here to express my thoughts.

I have a right to be here and I appreciate this opportunity.

The process of writing down our answers can be helpful — it can serve as a **visual reinforcement of our affirmations**.

What To Do Next?

Read your answers out loud, using a clear, proud voice.

It's best to **try this in a safe space, where you have privacy**. At home works well for a lot of people.

Then, ideally, you would **read your answers out loud again**, just a few moments **before you are going to speak up** to {insert name}.

This Can Give You an Extra Boost of Confidence.

Phew! You're done with this five-step process. You may feel like:

That was a lot of work!

But you know what…

You're worth it.

You're worth whatever effort and time it takes to stop fear dead in its tracks… to **make sure that fear doesn't stop you from what you want to say**.

WHAT'S NEXT?

RESOURCES… TO HELP YOU FIND WORK THAT YOU LOVE (and Stay Motivated and Inspired for the Journey…)

This Life Guide is "technically" finished, but I wanted to give you a few **more resources** on some **tricky work / career challenges** and on becoming **the BEST professional you can possibly be** … in case you want to continue to be inspired and lifted higher and higher (you won't even need that morning cup of coffee!)

Here are some of my favorites— articles and books I authored,[2] other Life Guides I created, and inspiring insights I shared when I was interviewed by a reporter from the Weekend Today Show.

Enjoy!

---

[2] All articles referenced in this section were published online.

TRICKY WORK / CAREER CHALLENGES

Job Hunting and Your Body: How to Walk Into Your Next Interview With Confidence, Even When You Don't Love How You Look
— Published on The Huffington Post.

http://www.huffingtonpost.com/dr-suzanne-gelb/jobhunting-your-body-how-_b_5624321.html#es_share_ended

Your Foolproof Guide to Moving on After You Messed Up at Work
— Published on my column "Be Well At Work", on the Muse.[3]

https://www.themuse.com/advice/your-foolproof-guide-to-moving-on-after-you-messed-up-at-work

Side note: The Muse is an award-winning online career resource, with over 4 million quality, professional members. I'm honored to have received the praise below, from Adrian Granzella Larssen, Editor-in-Chief, in response to an article that I wrote for The Muse:

"Wow! This is fantastic stuff. You're clearly incredible at what you do, and I'm so thrilled to share your advice with our audience!"

How to Deal With a Co-worker You Don't Like—But Everyone Else Is Obsessed With

---

[3] Except where otherwise noted, articles listed in this Resources section were published online in my column, "Be Well At Work" on The Muse.

https://www.themuse.com/advice/how-to-deal-with-a-coworker-you-dont-likebut-everyone-else-is-obsessed-with?ref=carousel-slide-0

How to Stop Obsessively Checking Your Work Email (and Stressing Yourself Out)

https://www.themuse.com/advice/how-to-stop-obsessively-checking-your-work-email-and-stressing-yourself-out

Your 3-Step Plan to Do Less at Work (But Make an Even Bigger Impact)

https://www.themuse.com/advice/your-3step-plan-to-do-less-at-work-but-make-an-even-bigger-impact

3 Ways to Get What You Need From Terrible Communicators — Published on TIME; originally published on my column "Be Well At Work" on The Muse

http://time.com/3768073/3-ways-get-from-terrible-communicators/

How to Get Over "Vacation Guilt" and Actually Enjoy Your Time Off

https://www.themuse.com/advice/how-to-get-over-vacation-guilt-and-actually-enjoy-your-time-off

Author's note:

So honored that The Muse featured my article about how to get over "Vacation Guilt" and actually enjoy time off, in their BEST OF THE WEB inspirational email on May 31, 2015.

Why Going "Above and Beyond" Can Hurt Your Career (and How to Break the Habit)

https://www.themuse.com/advice/why-going-above-and-beyond-can-hurt-your-career-and-how-to-break-the-habit?ref=search

How to Do a Great Job Even When You Don't Like Your Job

https://www.themuse.com/advice/how-to-do-a-great-job-even-when-you-dont-like-your-job

Should You Apply for That Slightly-Out-of-Reach Job—or Not?

https://www.themuse.com/advice/should-you-apply-for-that-slightlyoutofreach-jobor-not?ref=search

Allergic to Bragging? Try This Instead.

https://www.themuse.com/advice/allergic-to-bragging-try-this-instead

Should I Go to Grad School? 5 Questions to Make Sure it's the Right Move.

https://www.themuse.com/advice/should-i-go-to-grad-school-5-questions-to-make-sure-its-the-right-move

Are You Addicted to Your Job? 7 Ways to Tell

https://www.themuse.com/advice/are-you-addicted-to-your-job-7-ways-to-tell?ref=search

Drowning In The Details? How To Focus On Your Big Career Goals.

https://www.themuse.com/advice/drowning-in-the-details-how-to-refocus-on-your-big-career-goals

Emotional Outburst At Work? Here's How to Get Through It.
— Published online on The Huffington Post

http://www.huffingtonpost.com/dr-suzanne-gelb/outburst-at-work-sobbing-_b_7226214.html

Career Envy: What To Do When A Friend Gets The Job You Wanted.

https://www.themuse.com/advice/career-envy-what-to-do-when-a-friend-gets-the-job-you-wanted

How to Deal With Unreasonable Demands From Your Boss

https://www.themuse.com/advice/how-to-deal-with-unreasonable-demands-from-your-boss

4 Ways to Deal With an Office Crush

https://www.themuse.com/advice/4-ways-to-deal-with-an-office-crush

Spring Cleaning For Your Career: A Career Checklist
— Published on my column, "All Grown Up" on Psychology Today.

https://www.psychologytoday.com/blog/all-grown/201604/spring-cleaning-your-career-part-3-3

BECOMING THE BEST PROFESSIONAL YOU CAN BE

10 Ways Successful People Spend Their Time After Work

https://www.themuse.com/advice/10-ways-successful-people-spend-their-time-after-work?ref=carousel-slide-0

20 Career-Boosting Steps You Can Take Before New Year's Eve

https://www.themuse.com/advice/20-careerboosting-steps-you-can-take-before-new-years-eve?ref=carousel-slide-0

6 Self-Sabotaging Habits You Need To Drop Right Now
— Published on Mind Body Green.

https://www.mindbodygreen.com/0-14014/6-selfsabotaging-habits-you-need-to-drop-right-now.html

If You Want to Make Tomorrow Less Stressful—Start Tonight

https://www.themuse.com/advice/if-you-want-to-make-tomorrow-less-stressfulstart-tonight

Stressed Out at Work? How to Cope -- Without Turning to Food or Booze
— Published on the Huffington Post.

http://www.huffingtonpost.com/dr-suzanne-gelb/stressed-out-at-work-how-_b_6711034.html

You Are The Best Investment You'll Ever Make
— Published on my column, "All Grown Up," on Psychology Today.

https://www.psychologytoday.com/blog/all-grown/201511/you-are-the-best-investment-youll-ever-make

Why Positive Affirmations Don't Always Work (And What Does)
— Published on Tiny Buddah;

http://tinybuddha.com/blog/why-positive-affirmations-dont-always-work-and-what-does/

How to Succeed Everywhere: 10 Tips for Balance at Work, Home, in Relationships
— Written by Shelby Marra, published online on NBC's Today.

https://www.today.com/health/how-become-high-achieving-woman-work-your-relationship-parent-t33071

Side note: As my colleague, friend, and gifted writing teacher, Alex Franzen said: *"THIS IS AMAZING! Being interviewed by a reporter from NBC's Today Show? Uh, that's the big leagues!"*

Yes, that's what happened. Shelby Marra with NBC's Today Show in New York, requested an interview with me so that she could write this article featuring me, for TODAY.com's Successful Women series.

How Successful People Do More in 24 Hours Than the Rest of Us Do in a Week

— Published on Newsweek; originally published in my column, "Be Well At Work," on The Muse

https://www.newsweek.com/career/how-successful-people-do-more-24-hours-rest-us-do-week

What Your Résumé Looks Like To A Psychologist
— Published on Business Insider; originally published in my column, "Be Well At Work," on The Muse

http://www.businessinsider.com/what-your-rsum-looks-like-to-a-psychologist-2014-10

The Love Tune-Up: How to Amp Up the Love That's Naturally Inside You to Enjoy Happy, Healthy Relationships.

https://amzn.to/2UzTSP6

The Life Guide on How To Reach Your Ideal Weight — Through Kindness Not Craziness.

http://drsuzannegelb.com/life-guide-ideal-weight/

Praise for Dr. Gelb's Life Guides

"Learning how to love yourself and treat yourself kindly — even when your life, career, body, and relationships aren't 'totally perfect' — is one of the hardest things to do. Dr. Suzanne Gelb breaks down the art of self-love into practical steps. No woo-woo vagueness. Just easy-to-follow exercises pulled from her 28-year career in the field. If you're looking for practicality and effectiveness, these Life Guides are a steal of a deal."

—Susan Hyatt, Master Certified Life Coach, Published Author

"This Life Guide came at the perfect time. My two fears about losing weight were dispelled immediately and it was such a relief to know that I can start looking after myself without the worry of going to the gym or going on another desperate diet.

The audio helped re-frame the reasons why I've let my weight spiral out of control and the work book helped me set out an action plan. Thanks, Dr. Gelb, for your Life Guide, here's to a happier, healthier life."

—Amanda Herbert, photographer

"Dr. Gelb has a gentle spirit that instantly makes you feel like you've come home. The depth of her wisdom is undeniable, her curiosity is insatiable and her love is palpable. These qualities

make her the perfect guide for life. In the pages of the Life Guides you will find practical and proven processes to support you in living your great life. Whether it's heart-centered wisdom on navigating the dating world, love-based strategies for becoming a parent, or reaching your ideal weight through kindness, Dr. Gelb's Life Guides are gifts to be treasured."

— Dr. Gemma Stone, Psychologist, Mentor, Author

"Your guidebooks are gems."

—Alexandra Franzen, Published Author, Writing Teacher

ABOUT THE AUTHOR

Dr. Suzanne Gelb, Ph.D., J.D. is a psychologist, life coach, business consultant, and author. Over the past 30-plus years she has run her own business and helped people switch careers, get raises and promotions, launch new businesses (and more!).

Dr. Gelb's inspiring insights on personal growth have been featured on over 200 radio programs, 260 TV interviews, and online on Time, Newsweek, Forbes, The Huffington Post, NBC's Today, Business Insider, Psychology Today, Positively Positive, Mind Body Green, and many other places, as well.

Dr. Gelb's column, "Be Well At Work," featuring her writings on business-related topics, can be found on The Muse. This online platform attracts more than 75 million people each year, to help them be at the top of their game at work.

Dr. Gelb is the recipient of Small Business Booster (2000), one of Small Business Hawaii's Annual Business Awards.

She believes that it is never too late to become the person — and professional — you want to be. Strong. Confident. Calm. Creative. Free of all of the burdens that have held you back — no matter what has happened in the past.

To learn more, visit DrSuzanneGelb.com.

OTHER BOOKS BY THE AUTHOR

It Starts With You – How to Raise Happy, Successful Children by Becoming the Best Role-Model You Can Possibly Be. A Guidebook For Parents.

How to Get Your Kids to Cooperate and Help Them Become the Best Grown-Ups They Can Be. (A Life Guide.)

Helping Your Teen Make Healthy Choices About Dating and Sex. (A Life Guide.)

How to Get Ready to Be a Parent and Be the Best Mom or Dad You Can Possibly Be. (A Life Guide.)

How to Forgive the One Who Hurt You Most. (A Life Guide.)

How to Deal With People Who Drive You Absolutely Nuts. (A Life Guide.)

Aging With Grace, Strength and Self-Love. (A Life Guide.)

How to Navigate Being Single and Savor Your Dating Adventure. (A Life Guide.)

The Love Tune-Up: How to Amp Up the Love That's Naturally Inside You to Enjoy Happy, Healthy Relationships.

How to Rekindle That Spark and Create the Relationship and Sex Life That You Want. (A Life Guide.)

How to Reach Your Ideal Weight Through Kindness, Not Craziness. (A Life Guide.)

Welcome Home: Release Addictions and Return to Love.

How to Care for Yourself When You're a Caregiver for Somebody Else. (A Life Guide.)

Real Men Don't Vacuum. And Other Misguided Myths That Cause Conflict in Relationships.

INDEX[4]

A

affirmations, 45, 71, 78, 79, 93, 100
afraid, 20, 29, 58, 59, 66, 68, 69, 70, 71, 75, 76, 77, 83, 84, 85, 88
angry, 12, 28, 60
anxious, 60
ashamed, 12, 83
aspiration(s), 4, 5, 6, 7, 8, 41
avoiding, 63, 71

B

boredom, 21
boring, 9
boss, 11, 39, 92, 98
bright spots, 16
build confidence, 78
build your dream, 47, 49, 52
business, 1, 25, 45, 54, 55, 57, 59, 62, 78, 101, 104

C

calmer, 27, 85, 88
career, 2, 3, 4, 5, 7, 9, 14, 16, 17, 19, 20, 27, 28, 30, 32, 33, 41, 42, 45, 46, 50, 51, 52, 54, 60, 61, 66, 67, 69, 94, 95, 97, 98, 99, 101, 102
challenges, 25, 54, 94, 95
change(s), 1, 19, 24, 26, 28, 30, 44, 49, 53, 54, 64, 66, 69
children, 62, 63, 64, 85, 105
clients, 9, 11, 16, 23, 39, 54, 83, 85
colleagues, 12, 34, 39, 68
confidence, 46, 71, 78, 89, 90, 93, 95
confident, 72, 78, 104
conflict, 84, 106
conscious mind, 68
communication, 80, 81, 82
current job, 17, 18, 41
customers, 11, 39

D

deal breakers, 14
desires, 14, 68
different position, 41
discouraging, 4
dragging my feet, 55
dread, 72, 74

---

[4] The page numbers in this index refer to the printed version of this book.

dreams, 36, 44
dream career, 52

E

emotional inventory, 28
emotion(s), 3, 21, 26, 29, 68, 82, 87, 88
emotional workout, 87
enjoy, 18, 33, 38, 41, 42, 54, 94, 96, 97, 101, 105
excited, 51, 66, 72
exciting, 33
expectations, 68, 75

F

fear, 29, 55, 57, 58, 60, 61, 66, 67, 68, 72, 81, 82, 83, 84, 85, 87, 88, 89, 90, 91, 93
fear of failure, 55, 58, 61
fear of success, 66, 67, 68
feel good, 53
feel like quitting, 50
feel pressured, 68
feeling stuck, 72
fill in the blanks, 10, 18, 33, 37, 50, 75, 78, 91
frustrated, 20, 28, 69
frustrating, 4
frustrations, 10, 15, 23
fun, 23, 88

G

goals, 33, 36, 56, 57, 59, 62, 64, 98
gratifying, 17

H

happy, 5, 16, 17, 19, 20, 21, 22, 23, 30, 41, 61, 62, 71, 85, 101, 105
happy ending, 61, 62, 71
healing, 84, 87
high expectations, 68

I

industry, 1, 25
inner child, 88, 91
inspired, 3, 46, 94
inspiring, 27, 94, 104
intentions, 36, 55
internal conflict, 84

J

jealous, 13, 68

L

leave this job, 18
love your work, 3, 49

lucrative, 23

M

make a plan, 44
meaningful career, 3, 32
mindset, 26, 27
miserable, 19
miss out, 20
motivated, 63, 94

N

negative emotions, 26
nervous, 22
new job, 30, 71, 72, 80
new path, 2
not motivated, 63
nurture the child within, 88

O

options, 2, 19, 23, 24, 25, 26, 29
overwhelmed, 2, 19, 25, 47, 48

P

parenting skills, 65
patient, 50
patterns, 17, 19
perfectionist(s), 59, 60
pillow exercise, 29, 59, 85, 89

planning, 27
position, 1, 19, 25, 71
postpone, 74
positive change, 64
potential, 2, 11, 19, 66, 68
poor communicators, 80
preferences, 14
prime your mind, 27
procrastination, 55, 56, 57, 58, 59, 61, 62, 66, 64, 65, 69, 72, 73, 75
proud, 18, 32, 62, 93
put off, 55, 64, 74
putting it off, 63

R

relax, 20, 75, 86
resources, 94
risks, 6, 32

S

sad, 28
scared, 29
scream, 29, 85, 87
self-defeating, 56, 72
self-discipline, 56, 64
self-reflection, 10
self-respect, 52
self-sabotaging habit, 75, 99
similar job, 25
soothing self-talk, 90
soul-searching, 10
speaking up, 80, 81, 82, 88, 90, 91
strengthen confidence, 71, 89

stress, 9
stuck, 2, 66, 72, 106
subconscious, 58, 68

T

terrible communicators, 81, 96
take a risk, 2, 6, 32
too hard to change, 24
too late, 1, 2, 24, 45, 104

U

unhappy, 2, 9, 10, 16, 32
uplift your self-talk, 4
uplifting, 17, 54

V

visionary planning, 27
visualize, 85

W

workaholic, 68
worksheets, 4, 54
writing exercise, 10, 17, 37, 50, 54, 69, 70, 71, 72, 73, 78, 91, 92
wrong company, 1
wrong business model, 1

www.ingramcontent.com/pod-product-compliance
Lightning Source LLC
Chambersburg PA
CBHW020143130526
44591CB00030B/178